Stop Talking to Yourself
and
Start Listening

By Robin Schneider Larkin

SHIRES●PRESS
4869 Main Street
P.O. Box 2200
Manchester Center, VT 05255
www.northshire.com

Stop Talking to Yourself and Start Listening
©2016 by **Robin Schneider Larkin**
ISBN: 978-1-60571-308-3

Building Community, One Book at a Time
*A family-owned, independent bookstore in
Manchester Ctr., VT, since 1976 and Saratoga Springs, NY since 2013.
We are committed to excellence in bookselling.
The Northshire Bookstore's mission is to serve as a resource for
information, ideas, and entertainment while honoring the needs
of customers, staff, and community.*

Printed in the United States of America

Dedicated to my husband, Ed and our amazing daughter. Without her enthusiasm and his confidence there would be much less in my world.

Table of Contents

Introduction		page 1
Chapter 1	Personality	page 4
Chapter 2	Owning your life	page 14
Chapter 3	Introvert vs extrovert	page 24
Chapter 4	Maximizers vs satisficers	page 30
Chapter 5	Boundaries	page 36
Chapter 6	Mind reading – Don't	page 40
Chapter 7	No one makes you feel anything	page 44

Introduction

What qualifies me to write a self-help book? For fifteen years, I was in therapy and did a lot of inner work. It helped. I was twenty-seven and engaged to be married when I started therapy and that was probably ten years overdue. You might be asking why I waited so long. *This woman must be a slow learner*! That is partly true. My life was the way it was because I had found it worked…to some degree. We develop behaviors to overcome problems and weaknesses and they work for a while until they stop working. I read self-help books just like this one and did some learning and growing on my own. What I had to admit to myself was that I needed to raise the bar. I wanted a certain life. I just did not want to work at it. I wanted to live a comfortable life in the suburbs, but I didn't want my husband to travel for work or stay late at the office. I wanted to be considered smart, but I didn't want to get educated. I was creative but moving a sewing machine and fabric from apartment to apartment does not mean you are actually creating anything. Intention is great, but action is what gets the job done.

Maybe you are like me. I have this voice inside my head that can usually find a few good reasons not to do something. Or find ways to make what was wrong someone else's fault, because it certainly wasn't my fault. For years, my response to any dissatisfaction was to exclaim "I hate my life!" One day, I looked at myself in the mirror and said "If you hate your life so much, then change it." And slowly and methodically I did.

My life looks the same as it did before. I am still married to the same guy, still drive the same car and have the same job. The change came when I consciously decided to add pleasure and fulfillment to my life. New thoughts and a better awareness was the way to an authentic life. I had to stop talking to myself and start listening to what I needed. Was it scary at times? Sure. Moving out of your comfort zone is scary. It is also exhilarating and liberating. I found myself saying "If I can do this, then, I can do that." That's how I found the courage and perseverance to open my handwoven clothing business and at forty-four years of age finally earning my Bachelors of Arts degree. Or most surprising (to me, not to those who know me now) is the fact I'm a graduate school student.

It is my belief that when we engage in therapy or any attempt to craft a better life we are on a sort of archeology dig. As we and/or our therapist sweep away the dirt and debris of lives, pieces emerge with broken and jagged edges and we have to figure out where they belong. Sometimes a piece seems to fit in one spot. But after a little more digging we discover it actually belongs in another spot or to another person altogether. We have to dig deep to find all the pieces and complete the puzzle. The process of understanding ourselves and living the most productive and satisfying lives possible will take time. It is important to be patient and deliberate. Those pieces are broken for a reason. While putting those puzzle pieces back together can be time consuming, the end result is worth it.

Chapter 1

Personality

The Oxford Dictionary defines Personality as "the combination of qualities or characteristics that form an individual's distinct character." There are many different theories of personality (Carver & Scheier, 2012). In other words, a lot of people have researched where personality and its different facets originate. Some researchers believe in a biological origin while others feel personality is shaped by our motives or by our childhood. Many people think their personality comes from their family of origin through genetics, while others think it is learned (Carver & Scheier, 2012). I think personality is both inherited and learned. I believe that our personality traits are consistent over time, but can be modified to achieve a more fulfilling life. Before you can modify you need to research and understand your own distinct personality.

You may have some insights into your personality already. Or you may be living your life according to someone else's personality quirks. Either way, the place to begin is by studying your personality. The foundation of my theory for living a fulfilling and satisfying life is to know yourself – the authentic you. Know what makes you tick, what makes you upset, what excites you, what makes you feel good and what makes you feel bad. You need to know what you need to feel content and safe.

This information is discoverable inside a study of your personality.

There are many ways to study your personality. Since others have done a lot of work in this area we can rely on their study guides for our journey. A good place to start is the free personality test found on the Keirsey website: www.keirsey.com. There are others. The point is to ask questions and gain knowledge.

In 2005, I took the Keirsey free Temperament Sorter. I was defined as an Idealist Champion. Some of the defining characteristics of an Idealist Champion include: "They see life as an exciting drama;" "They want to experience all the meaningful events and fascinating people in the world;" and a very important one, "Champions are constantly scanning the social environment."

At that time, I was struggling in my relationships and found the Keirsey Temperament Sorter a good place to begin to look for avenues of improvement. Reading the website's definition of the Idealist Champion personality did two things for me. First, I felt validated. I had gone through life longing to fill my life with new experiences which put me at odds with my husband who was happy with the status quo. I bored easily and hated time spent sitting around. Second, the definition validated some of my husband's complaints about life with me. I am "constantly scanning the social environment" and always looking for new and different experiences. I put a lot of responsibility on him for my unhappiness because I found life boring. The description begins by stating that Idealist Champions are rare: 3-4% of the population. So, the odds that my husband was also an Idealist Champion was unlikely and his aversion to the constant new and different confirmed that. Whether it came to me in a light bulb moment or slowly over time the end result was the same. I stopped expecting my husband to dance to life just like me. Gone was that unattainable picture of married bliss where he chased rainbows with me. No, if I wanted and needed to chase rainbows then I needed to do it on my own time. This took a big pressure off my marriage. Both of these realizations improved my life immediately.

After studying my personality evaluation, I took a long hard look at my life. Chasing experiences and drama all the time is exhausting. And a lot of those experiences and drama did not add much to life so I began to modify. I thought about what I wanted my life to look like on the everyday and over the course of time. And I looked at what held me back.

I wanted to learn new skills and began hobbies like kayaking and writing, but I was filled with fears -- some rational and some irrational. Take kayaking. I loved the idea of gliding through the water in a kayak. The problem was that I did not live on a body of water or own a kayak. I needed to rent one, strap it to the roof of my car and take it to a nearby lake. Where then I could glide through the water happily. Problem one: I don't like talking on the phone and would need to in order to reserve a kayak. Problem two: I envisioned the kayak flying off the top of my car on the highway. Problem three: How stupid would I look paddling? I was finally able to see these three problems as surmountable obstacles to something I felt would add a lot to my life. First, I saw it as a challenge and second as a happy way for a Pisces to spend an afternoon. There is nothing I like more than being near water. So, I challenged myself. I picked up the phone and called a local sporting goods store that rented kayaks. I reserved one. My daughter and I headed to the store the next day. I was nervous, but I kept telling myself people did this all the time so why not me? When the salesman helped me load the kayak on my car I peppered him with questions. He seemed unconcerned with my fears as he showed me how to tighten the straps, all four of them. We headed out of the parking lot toward our launch site. I was scared and refused to take the highway. I drove back roads preferring the longer, but slower, ride to a faster and in my mind, more dangerous drive. But the important thing was that I did it. When we got to the lake my daughter and I managed to take the kayak off the car without injury. It was a bit of a challenge but not insurmountable. Before long we were seated together in our kayak paddling across the water.

Kayaking was everything I thought it would be. I loved it from the start. Seven years later, I still get a little anxious every time I pull out of my driveway with my kayak strapped to the top of my car. I have to talk to myself as I pull onto the highway, challenging those irrational fears of the kayak flying off the car. But the important thing is I recognized kayaking is important to me. I need to continue to challenge the voice in my head that attempts to thwart my kayaking adventures. Every time I go out kayaking it is a new experience fulfilling my personality's needs.

In 2013, when I revisited the Keirsey Temperament Sorter things turned more interesting. Eight years and a lot of work had changed my personality result. I am now an Idealist Counselor. I feel it's a kinder, gentler Idealist than the Champion. I am still seeking out new experiences but now it is about growth instead of drama. As I said in the opening paragraph, I think some personality traits are inherited and some are learned. I have inherited a curious mind. I love talking to people and learning something new. This is both inherited and learned. My whole family is like that. We strike up conversations with people wherever we go. Not everyone has that inherent trait nor was everyone raised in as curious a family as I was. Embracing who you are is important. Embracing the differences of those who reside in your world is also important. Don't apologize for who you are. At the same time don't make someone apologize for who they are.

I know there are people out there who do not have a computer or who choose not to use websites. I would still encourage you to research your personality. The following quiz can be used to augment the Keirsey test and it is useful on its own. Taking a long hard look at oneself can sometimes bring up painful or embarrassing parts of our personality. Most of us would like to be sociable, empathetic and caring individuals. Not all of us are. And that is okay. Working with your personality allows you to embrace all the parts of yourself and learn to love them. It also gives you a chance to modify them.

A good place to start is by taking a look at your day-to-day life. Since, my goal for you is to create a life tailor written to your specifications this is the perfect place to start. How does your day begin? For example, I am a get right out of bed when the alarm goes off and get started with my day kind of person. My husband, on the other hand, wakes up slowly and if possible will take thirty minutes to get out of bed. This used to cause some friction between us because I thought he was lazy and he thought I was a nag. Now, I get up and start my day while he sleeps in and neither feels the need to critique each other's style. I may get more done by 9AM than he does, but he gets his work done by the end of the day. (and if he doesn't it is not my problem). For a long time, these two styles created disharmony between us because he felt abandoned on a Saturday morning when I would choose to get up and write, work out or cook rather than snuggle with him. In turn, I considered him a lazy dog for lolling around in bed. Now, I get up quietly and start my day then come back to bed an hour later and snuggle with him. We hit the day together from there. It took communication to accomplish this and an understanding that neither one of us was wrong. This is crucial. Just because someone behaves differently from you does not make them wrong.

Back to your day- to- day life: work your way through it. Where you live, how long your commute is, how/where/what you eat, how you communicate, who you interact with. These are all important things to consider. Take notice of what makes you feel good and what makes you feel bad. Be careful here. It is easy to think that because you have a hard time getting up in the morning and dread starting your day that you dislike your job. But maybe it's your morning routine or your commute that has you pulling up the covers when the alarm goes off. Maybe you think you hate your apartment because of your noisy neighbors, but the reality is you are jealous of those partying people and wish you felt comfortable entertaining.

The goal with this exercise is to understand what makes you think, feel or behave the way you do. Your personality will provide consistent reactions to various experiences from the everyday to the special occasion (Carver & Scheier, 2012). The study of personality is large and complex. Researchers have attempted to narrow personality down to five areas in the Five Factor Model. Even though they managed to come up with a title for their model, researchers over the decades have not been able to agree on titles for each factor. The factors also differ by culture. (Carver & Scheier, 2012). For the purposes of this book, I have used a combination of categories and definitions that provide a good jumping off place for you to explore your personality. On a separate sheet of paper answer these questions.

Ponder your Personality

Sociability means how social do you like to be? Some people will think of extrovert versus introvert but that is a subject I tackle in Chapter three in a way in which you might not be familiar.

- Describe your favorite way(s) to spend a free day or night.
    - How do you feel afterwards?
- How often do you do your favorite activities?
- Do you have people who you enjoy spending time? Is there a group or do you prefer one on one exchanges?

Emotional stability refers to your interactions with others and experiences.

- Do you tend to be nervous and excitable or calm cool and collected?
- If someone criticizes or critiques you, how much does this upset you, if at all?
- How much time do you spend worrying about things both vague and specific?

Agreeableness refers to how important you place politeness and the consideration of others in your interactions with others.

- Do you like to be seen as warm and considerate of others?
- Does your everyday life allow this level of warmth?
- Do the important people in your life share your level of agreeableness?

Conscientiousness has two sides to it. One is how much of a planner versus how spontaneous you are. The other refers to how hardworking you are.

- Describe your ideal workday.
- Describe your ideal relaxing day.

Inquiring intellect also refers to two parts: intellect and openness to experience. These are two sides of the same coin in that how much you enjoy being challenged is a part of your personality.

- Do you enjoy learning new things, trying new foods, meeting new people and visiting new places?
- If you do enjoy the new and different, is it a challenge for you or do you easily move into the unknown?
- Regardless of your answer to the above questions in what new ways can your life reflect those answers?

After you answer the questions, sit with your thoughts for a while. Go do something else and let it percolate. Does anything else come up? It's easy when we are unhappy to jump to big changes. Instead, I encourage you to make smaller changes over time. The smaller changes may lead to big changes like a move or a new job or the smaller changes may lead to a more fulfilling life within the core boundaries of your present life. When we understand what is intrinsically important to us we can make a concentrated effort to incorporate those things into our lives. This will increase the fulfillment factor and decrease that nagging sense that something in our lives is missing.

Chapter 2

Owning Your Life

I want to see change in my life, but he/she won't change for me! Does this sound familiar? So often, we can list tons of changes we would like the people around us to make, but rarely do we look at the actual agent of change in our lives: ourselves. It's been said that the only person you can change is yourself and this is unequivocally true. Even if someone were to make all those changes you requested there is still one thing left unchanged: you. A better place to begin to make changes is in our own lives. But how?

My favorite expression for years was "I hate my life". And I could give numerous reasons why it was all everyone else's fault. Finally, about 8 years ago, even I got tired of listening to myself complain about my life. I looked at myself in the mirror and said "Then change it if you hate it so much." And so I did. Little changes gave me the courage to make bigger changes and I can honestly say that now I love my life. It doesn't look that different now than eight years ago: same husband, daughter, main job (mom and housewife) and location. But I stopped waiting for my husband to change. I stopped waiting for him to want to come along on the adventures I wanted to take. Now, I invite him to join me on my adventures but it does not matter if he comes along or not. I craft my day to my specifications and not to someone else's.

To be satisfied in your life, you must feel comfortable taking charge of your life. I know so many people who really struggle with advocating for their own needs. Because of the losses I have endured in my life, I am wholly aware that we don't know how long we have in this world. I feel it is crucially important to make every day significant. My sister was killed by a drunk driver when she was 27 years old and I was eleven. My father developed Alzheimers Disease right around the time he retired. His retirement was what he lived for his entire working life. Because of his illness he got maybe five good years to enjoy. I live my life in the now because I know the future is uncertain. However, I know I may get to live to 85 or 90 so I live my life with intention and an eye to the future. There is a fine line between immediate gratification and enjoying every day to the maximum.

As I said, I spent many years hating my life. I blamed others for not dancing to the music in my head and the world for not conforming to my needs and desires. Two things happened to change this mind set. I had a bit of a light bulb moment after a fight with a friend. We hung up on each other because I was mad that he changed his mind about going out. I was free and I wanted my friend to ignore his own needs and wants and take care of mine. I had to face the harsh truth that the person I thought I was and the person I acted like were not the same, painful observation number one. But that was not all. I also sat and thought about what I really wanted to do that evening. Painful observation #2 was that I had gotten boring. On my free nights, I usually went out to hear music and drink, which was why I needed my friend to pick me up. By the following day my viewpoint had changed. When I thought about what I really wanted to do with my evening I decided to make a bowl of popcorn and curl up on the couch and watch TV. I wanted to hunker down and regroup. And the next day I wanted to have the energy (and not a hangover) to go out and explore some new hiking paths.

I allowed myself to consciously construct what I wanted my weekend to look like. I had the house to myself and was free to do whatever I wanted. Instead of falling back on the same old habits, I made some popcorn and curled up on the couch with the remote. I thought about how many of my friends would have loved to have an evening to themselves. I had no one to cook for but myself, no one argued with me about my choice of shows and I could go to bed whenever I wanted. I began to feel positive and grateful. I listened to myself and found a new plan that felt right and authentic.

To develop your authentic life, you need to learn to challenge your long- or even short -held beliefs. Challenge your thoughts. Don't believe the first thing that pops into your head.

The next day while packing a picnic lunch for my hike I got nervous again. I considered cancelling my plan to go to the new park and instead hiking the same old trail I had followed many times before. But I really wanted to explore a new place. So I listened to my fears and made the conscious decision to override them. I went to the new park and had a blast by myself.

That weekend I learned that I was responsible for my life and my happiness and it mattered how I handled it. As I said in the last chapter I was defined as an Idealist Champion which makes ups only three to four percent of the population (Keirsey.org). Your issues and long held beliefs are probably going to be different than mine. But both the thought and the action processes are the same. It is your life. What do you want it to look like?

Many people think that those in a happy relationship do everything alike and together. Some do. But many don't. If you are single you may keep getting the message that you need to be in a relationship. If you want to be in a relationship, then actively take steps to add people to your life who could become your life partner. If a relationship is not important to you then enjoy your single life. If you are in a relationship with a person who loves the country life and adores the town you both live in while you keep having fantasies about running away to the city then you have a lot of thinking to do. I personally do not think anyone is worth sacrificing your happiness for nor do I think it ever works out long term. If you are honest with your partner though, (and yourself) maybe a compromise could be reached.

When we lived in New Hampshire, I was shocked at the number of people who hated the cold and snow. If you are not familiar with New Hampshire, let me tell you that freezing temperatures and snow traditionally last for half the year. That's a large block of time that they were unhappily gazing out the window. I asked people why they lived in New Hampshire if they hated the weather so much and their answer usually involved growing up there or marrying someone who actually did love the cold, snow and sports associated with the weather. If you are in that situation, complaining may seem like your only option. It certainly is a popular one, but you have other options.

I am cold all winter. I have less than ideal circulation and my hands and feet literally feel like ice for much of the winter (ask my husband). However, I love winter and was one of the few people who was a bit sad to see this past one end. The key to my winter happiness: finding winter activities I enjoy in the snow and cold that actually warm me up. First I tried snowshoeing and that was pretty good. It's easy and cheap and gets me outside where I am happiest. Then, my daughter learned to cross country ski in gym class. I asked her to teach me. (If you want to score points with your pre-teen or teen: ask them to teach you how to do something). We had a blast. Well, I had a blast. She was a little annoyed that I didn't fall once on my first time out and she, the teacher, fell a lot. I used to downhill ski so I think that's why it came to me quicker. Now, I am eagerly anticipating those winter snowstorms and getting out the minute I am free to slide across the winter wonderland. And it warms me up – hand and feet too! But not everyone can embrace outdoor winter sports. And not everyone can uproot their family to warmer climates.

That's the goal of the next questionnaire. What would make your difficult time of the year easier? There are so many indoor sport facilities now: rock climbing gyms, racquetball and tennis clubs. Cheaper and less strenuous: write that novel you always felt was inside you or that book of poetry. Or just curl up in your favorite chair with a good book after you struggle through another messy winter commute. The key is to hear what your body and mind tell you. Honor those thoughts and feelings. Then do something positive and productive about it. This is where good communication skills come in to play. You don't have to be the same person doing the same things all year round because people expect that of you. Articulate how difficult certain times of the year are for you and ask for help from your children and your partner. Give yourself a break. How we deal with life's adversities and joys is our own choice. Allow yourself the freedom to choose.

I would always encourage small steps first, though. Save the big life- altering steps for last. There is a lot of knowledge to be discovered in little steps. The following questionnaire is designed to take the information you have discovered thus far and add to it. You are starting to formulate a game plan for yourself. Have fun with it!

Write your own life script – after all it is your life.

On a separate sheet of paper, write down your ideas and thoughts to the questions below. This is your vision for your life. Don't complicate it with stipulations or stringent considerations. Picture what you want your life to look like and write it down. It's your vision so use words or pictures or a combination of both. Create a collage, a poem, a list or an essay. The important thing is to be honest and forthright. Changes can't happen unless we communicate our thoughts effectively.

Daily Life:

- How do you want your morning to look? What time do you get up? Does it allow you ample time to do the things you want to do?

- Look at your daily routine. What parts are there only to please others? What isn't there because it only pleases you?

- Is there enough music, dance, exercise, reading, downtime and pleasure or do you feel like you are on a treadmill of drudgery? Where can you add pleasurable activities?

- Do your meals nourish your body and soul? Or do they only nourish the body or only the soul? Healthy food doesn't have to be expensive and it can taste good too.

Monthly life:

- What do your weekends look like?

- What do you want your weekends look like?

- What have you wanted to try and never found the time, courage or money to do?

- What do you love to do and do you make time for it on a regular basis?

- What are some goals you can set for yourself?

Yearly life:

- Where do you see yourself in one year or five years? Where do you want to see yourself?

- Some goals take time to put into motion. Are you making real progress towards yours?

- What daily and monthly steps can you take towards your bigger goals?

- Break it down. Where do you want to be in a month? Three months? Six months? Nine months? One year? Three years? Five years? Think financially, health wise, career wise and personally.

This is your life. To achieve happiness, you need to describe the life you want. Then sit with it. Then figure out ways to get there.

Chapter 3

Introvert vs Extrovert

I hope as you put together your thoughts in the preceding chapters you saw trends or patterns emerge. This chapter will tie those behavioral patterns to the following concept: whether you are an extrovert or an introvert. It is important to be clear when using words with multiple definitions. In this chapter, the term extrovert and introvert are defined in accordance with the book *Raising your Spirited Child* (2006). The author uses the concepts extrovert or introvert to describe how each of us gets our energy. Extroverts derive their energy from other people. Introverts' energy banks are filled by being alone. How we acquire energy is a characteristic we are born with and not one we learn. To make changes that will improve how our relationships function, we must determine whether we and our loved ones are introverts or extroverts.

I learned this concept when my daughter was young and it was enormously helpful to me as a parent, partner and individual. It was just as valuable for me to assess my daughter's and husband's placement on this spectrum as it was to do it for myself. I'll give you an example. A number of years ago, after I had been incorporating this idea into our family life we attended a state fair. Even though I am an extrovert, a state fair with all its crowds and noises is my worst nightmare. My husband is an introvert but he loves the fair's rides and food. The noise and people do not bother him. Our daughter is an extrovert but noises and crowds can also bother her. However, she loves amusement park rides, the scarier the better. When we got in the car to drive home, I sat in the passenger side and my husband sat in the driver's seat, as usual. We pulled onto the highway. My husband and daughter chatted about their favorite rides and I enjoyed their conversation now that I was away from the incessant noise. About fifteen minutes into the drive I saw that my husband was fighting to stay awake. I quickly suggested he pull over. He did and we switched seats. He was asleep before I had driver a mile. I, on the other hand, was full of energy and happy to listen to the radio while I drove us home. At home, we talked about it and realized this was a common occurrence. When we spend the day out, specifically in a crowded place like the city or a festival my husband needs to sleep on the way home. Since I have completely filled my energy bank by being around people, I am full of energy and drive us home.

Now that we've figured it out, we have created a great system. We looked back and saw how many times this had happened, recognized it as a pattern and made positive changes. Another example of changes in our family that occurred when my husband recognized that whenever our daughter and I have spent too much time hanging out at home we start dragging emotionally and physically. He makes positive change by suggesting an outing that will refill our energy banks.

Remember that being an extrovert or an introvert is a genetic characteristic (Kurcinka, 2006) and not something you can train yourself out of. It is something to manage but not a failing or an insurmountable obstacle to a life dream. Kids who are introverts simply come home from school and spend time alone for a while to regroup. They are still able to manage their school day and be successful. I learned I could not use a time out in her room as a punishment. It was sheer agony for her to be alone on a different floor from everyone else. I found another strategy that worked but was not as debilitating.

Introverts and extroverts communicate in different ways. The author of *Raising your Spirited Child* explains that introverts want to share their thoughts and ideas after careful consideration and in small doses. Extroverts, on the other hand, have a lot to say and will rarely take a break unless it is requested. This difference in communication style has caused my husband and me numerous problems over the years. I would get annoyed and insulted when he wouldn't respond right away to my new ideas. I would think my thoughts were not important to him. On the contrary, they were very important to him. He wanted to think through his response and get back to me in a day or two when he was ready. By then, I, the extrovert had already moved on to the next idea. This problem leads to another concept: Don't try to read someone's mind. We will cover this in another chapter.

Finding out whether you are an introvert or an extrovert speaks to the importance of two things: knowing yourself and understanding that we are all different. When we take the time to learn how we best operate, we can then approach life from our most productive and positive place. I worked successfully from home as a weaver for nine years. Yes, as an extrovert I spent large chunks of time holed up in my studio. But I also made sure to spend time out in the community. I actually enjoyed food shopping because it gave me a chance to refuel my energy bank. Are there better ways to do that? Sure, but it never hurts to put a positive spin on a chore! I also had to remind myself when I would get sad or tired that it was not the work necessarily that was getting me down but the lack of human contact. This piece of the puzzle is just as important if you are involved in any kind of relationship. My husband understands how important it is for my mental health that I get out of the house so he encourages me to go out without him. I understand he isn't trying to get rid of me. It's actually a very thoughtful gift. Introverts and extroverts can successfully create a happy fulfilling life together as long as they honor each other's differences.

Take a few minutes to think about your favorite ways to spend time. And how do you spend that time?

- When you are at a party do you find yourself talking to everyone there? Or do you find a kindred spirit and spend most of the time chatting with them? Are you the first one to arrive and one of the last to leave? Or do you drag your feet and arrive late and leave early?
- Do you have lots of friends or just a few close confidantes?
- When you go see a movie do you spend the hours afterwards debating and discussing what you have seen? Or do you sit with what you have viewed and mull it over for days?

When my family gets together (all fifteen of us), by the end of the night my two sisters in law and my husband are fighting over who will do the dishes ----in the quiet kitchen ---- alone. I used to get annoyed with my husband for hiding out in the kitchen during parties. Now I understand he needs to refill his energy bank after talking all day with a roomful of extroverts! I think this is the hardest part: understanding that what someone does is not against you but for them. Although, equally hard is doing for ourselves instead of doing what we think everyone expects of us. Either way, a conflict with another person results in a lesson. Take the time to puzzle out the pieces and learn about yourself. Be gentle and understanding with yourself and others as you work through what everyone needs.

Chapter 4

Maximizers vs Satisficers

My journey has had some really annoying turns. Like when I learned that all that time I had been spending on making good solid decisions was actually not increasing the satisfaction in my life. Weighing the pros and cons of each option and searching for the best possible choice is a trait I come by genetically. It took my father two years to buy me a bike. Literally, two years to pick out a bike. Now, the fact that I was driving my brothers' hand- me- down from fifteen years prior should have been a motivating factor and maybe it was. For all I know my mom could have put her foot down and said "Pick one!" Unlikely, but possible. I still have the bike by the way. I recently got it back on the road and it still rides great. My father was a maximizer and all of his kids are as well.

In a positive psychology class, I learned that the world of decision making can be divided into maximizers and satisficers (Peterson, 2006). Maximizers look to make the very best choice out of all the options available. Satisficers make "good enough" choices. In the bike example, my father was a maximizer and my best friend's Dad who went to the local big box store and bought his daughter the ten speed bike on sale was a satisficer. She probably doesn't still have the bike, but she did have it two years sooner! Obviously, there are some decisions you should take your time with like getting married or buying a house. Decisions about what kind of toilet paper to buy or where to go to dinner should not take hours to process. Pick one and move on.

Hopefully the following information will motivate you to ditch your need to compare everything. Research has shown that maximizers take longer to decide but gain less satisfaction from their decisions (Peterson, 2006). This is the piece that can enhance your life. If you are sweating over all the choices open to you: career, college, relationships, vacation and shopping it is time to take a look at your decision making process and make some changes. As I said, this was one of those aha moments that took me out of my comfort zone.

My husband jokes that when we are on vacation I am thinking about lunch while we are eating breakfast and thinking about dinner while we are eating lunch. Picking a restaurant for date night was a grueling process after our daughter was born. What did I feel like eating? What did he feel like eating? What restaurants were agreeable to both of us? It had to be fancy enough for date night but not too expensive. So many criteria! The dining experience rarely lived up to my expectations. And date night never lived up to either of our expectations because we were too busy dealing with my disappointment. I spent so much time trying to maximize my choice there was no way it could live up to my vision.

A therapist finally honed in on my crippling desire to maximize every decision. Our homework after one session was to go out on a date night, but I had to let my husband pick the restaurant and I could say nothing except "Sounds great!" That first time, it nearly killed me. But I thought about the points she had made: we weren't just going out for a meal. We were spending quality time alone together. The conversation should be more important than the menu. I learned quite the lesson in being satisfied with good enough. When we arrived at the restaurant my husband had picked there was a 30 minute wait. We left and continued to a nearby city with tons of good restaurants. He picked another place. Another thirty minute wait. We went to two more restaurants with the same response. In the old days, my maximizing ways would have had me livid. But I focused my energy on what was important. Before we walked into the next place I said, "If there is a wait, we'll eat at the bar. We never do that. It'll be fun." Hubby agreed. And so we ate at the bar. Was it perfect? Could we have had a better meal at the bar of one of those other restaurants? Maybe. But that wasn't what mattered. What mattered was that we did something different and had fun together.

My dinner story has a positive ending but the problem was real and was damaging to our relationship. I have learned it's impossible to maximize every aspect of my life. I have learned to be happy with how things turn out regardless of how I pictured them. I have learned over the years that the washer and dryer we bought after I maximized the decision lasted no longer than the washer and dryer I bought impulsively at the first store I went in to. Some of it was learning to trust my intuition or my instincts. Some of it was breaking old habits. And a lot of it was letting go of a need to have no regrets. In life, we may have regrets but we do not need to hold them close and reexamine each and every one in detail.

If any of this sounds familiar, I encourage you to take a look at your decision making process. Maximizing every decision could be keeping you from enjoying your life fully. Take a moment to write down some of your more recent decisions both big and small. Did it take you almost as long to choose your vacation destination as it did to order the toppings on your Friday night pizza? Then maybe it's time to prioritize your time.

Are you a maximizer or a satisficer?

To determine whether you are a mazimizer, one who tries to make the very best choice out of all the options available, or a satisficer, one who makes "good enough" choices, please answer the following questions on a separate sheet of paper.

- Most recent decision I made.

- How long did it take?

- How happy I was with the outcome?

- Decision I see in my future?

- Should I Maximize or Satisfice it?

- Why?

- After the decision is made write down how you feel about your decision.

Chapter 5

Boundaries

In this chapter, I discuss boundaries. When I refer to boundaries, I mean the invisible dividing line between what is appropriate and what is not appropriate. What is appropriate and inappropriate is different for everyone. Each person has their own boundary lines. Some have different boundaries for different people. They will talk about certain things or allow certain behaviors with some people but not others. Some individuals have no boundaries. For them, nothing is off limits. Some individuals have trouble setting boundaries with the people in their life. If you are one of these people, then this chapter is for you.

I conquered boundary setting a long time ago. I understood the importance of being clear with people on how far is too far or what my expectations are in different situations. For a long time, I have had a three strike and you are out rule. I am not a baseball fan, but I think the concept works. Three strikes allows me to let people know where I stand and give them a chance to work with me. For example, I had a friend who liked to tell jokes that made fun of people (ethnically, politically). I told him that I did not like it and to please not tell those types of jokes in my presence. That was his first strike.

Boundary setting is about serious things. It's about situations that make you uncomfortable or are in conflict with your value system. I have a serious problem with people who need to get a laugh or look good by stepping on others. That was why this was a strike situation. The second time my friend told an inappropriate joke it was in my home. I reminded him that I am offended by those types of jokes and followed up with, "Don't tell them in my home." That was his second strike. Luckily, it only took two strikes and this person understood the boundary line and decided our friendship was more important than crossing that line again.

I have had to go to three strikes especially when I was dating. When you are dating someone, you should look for deal breakers. Deal breakers are those things that you just can't abide. Those are pretty easy. Someone steals something from a store or doesn't tip a service person and you know right off: deal breaker. But it is harder to make a call on some behavior. Maybe you really like the person except for this one trait. They are always late or call and cancel last minute because of work. Being a committed worker is a positive, but when someone uses their job to inconvenience you it becomes a negative. In this type of situation you can utilize the three strike rule. The next time your date shows up late or cancels last minute because of work tell them it's not okay because it has become a pattern of behavior. Set the boundary that your feelings are as important as the job. If you don't set the boundary and marry this person and they miss out on the birth of their child because of "the job," you really can't complain. You didn't set that boundary.

Boundary setting is helpful in awkward situations with friends as well. Maybe you have that friend who constantly complains about her boyfriend who also happens to be your friend. It makes you really uncomfortable and you've asked her to stop, but she doesn't. Employ the three strikes rule. I use three strikes because as I once said to a boyfriend, "Perhaps you didn't understand me the first time but this is a deal breaker, and if you can't respect my boundary on it then we're done." That was for the second strike. The third strike doesn't require much communication other than "We're done." said directly after the offensive behavior. With friends, especially long term friends, it can be harder to be that black and white. If the idea of losing your friend over a boundary issue seems wrong, then revisit the issue. Ask yourself: Is this issue worth losing this friend over? Can you and the friend reach some sort of compromise or understanding?

People will argue against your boundary settings both as you set and defend them. At times, it is awkward to explain to a friend that what they are doing is outside of your value system. But the alternative is worse: devaluing yourself. When we set boundaries, we let others know that our feelings and thoughts have value. *We* have value. By extension, when our friends knowingly show disrespect for our feelings they do not value us. Do you really want to waste your time on someone who does not value you?

We don't all share the same values. We don't all have the same needs. Some people would have no problem with friends consistently being late or canceling at the last minute. For them, it's not a problem. That is why this is an important, sometimes difficult concept to master. By setting boundaries, there are no hidden traps for people to fall into causing anger or disappointment. Time and energy are not wasted on miscommunications or misunderstandings. Open communication between two people means there are no hidden resentments to erode the framework of the relationship.

Chapter 6

Mind reading – Don't

When my husband and I first got together we always said to each other "Get out of my head!" It was cute and true. He would say something that I had just been thinking. Or I would suggest something and he would have been about to suggest the same thing. We thought we could reach into each other's minds. This was bad because we stopped communicating. We always thought we knew what the other person was thinking so we didn't need to talk to each other. We didn't need to explain our thoughts or plans or actions. There was only one problem. No one can read your mind.

Some people do know what you're thinking sometimes. A certain old friend and I can go out and have a whole conversation without saying a word. But when we need to make a decision we open our mouths and talk. I know what she likes to eat but I still ask, "Where do you want to go for dinner?" I don't assume.

Dinner is one thing, but what about the big stuff? What about that guy you're dating who you think is "the one." Does he want kids? How many? Day care or not? Suburbs or a farm in the middle of nowhere? Does he know you really like spending the holidays away on tropical islands? Or that spending the holidays in your hometown is the only way you can imagine the holidays? Does he really hate his Dad or was he just blowing off steam? There are a million different ways to live a life. Don't assume because you look alike and were raised in the same type of setting you want the same things. Learn to talk about the little stuff and the big stuff become easier to discuss as well.

That covers relationships. How about everyday life? I hear people say things like "She knows I hate it when she talks to me like that" or "I can tell he's pissed at me." These are examples of someone using mind reading rather than communication. No one knows what you are thinking unless you tell them. On the flip side, you do not know what someone else is thinking unless you ask them. As for someone being pissed at you, lots of things can contribute to that person's behavior: being overwhelmed with work, irritated with the commute or not feeling well. You think your friend is mad at you so you avoid him hoping it will blow over. But the reality is he is overwhelmed at work and you are ignoring a friend in need.

Communication is a two way street. It's simple. Don't assume, ask. "Are you pissed at me or just the world in general?" "I guess I haven't told you before but I really don't like it when you take that tone with me." Well, the words are easy. Saying them can be hard. When we communicate with people we open ourselves up to them. That person may actually be pissed at you.

They may not care that you don't like their tone. On the other hand, you may find out their distance was because they are overwhelmed with work or family problems and by giving them a chance to talk about it you have just deepened the relationship. They may not even realize that they have a "tone" and are sorry they hurt your feelings thereby enhancing the friendship.

Communicating with someone about things that matter like, "How many kids do you want?" or "Where shall we live when we get married?" can be scary. But finding yourself on a cul-de-sac in the suburbs when you yearn for wide open spaces is scarier, especially when you add kids to the mix. This goes back to the first chapter. What do you want your life to look like? This chapter follows up on that question: Share what you want in your life with those in your world. They can't read your mind.

The following questions will help you work on your communication skills.

- What topics do you avoid discussing with loved ones?
- Do you think your partner shares your view of life? Have you asked them?
- After working on the questions in chapter two, did you share your findings with your loved one? Were they surprised by some or all of your thoughts?

- Do you ever use the expression "That's how everyone thinks/acts!" Do you believe that everyone thinks the way you do?
- If you are less communicative than you would like, do you think you can improve your communication skills? Are you worried about how people will receive your message?
- What about sharing with others makes you uncomfortable?

Chapter 7

No one makes you feel anything

"You make me feel so _____!" If this is something you say often then this is your chapter. We sometimes blame others for how we feel in their company. But the reality is that you are responsible for your own feelings. My husband used to complain about my housecleaning. Keeping a neat and tidy house is not my priority. I am an artist. The mess is comfortable and only begins to get to me every few weeks. When the chaos begins to create chaos in my mind, I sweep through the house and put everything back into its proper place. To me, a messy house is a comfortable house and I want my guests to feel comfortable. My husband, on the other hand wants a sparkling clean house when guests are expected. I used to feel insulted and bad about myself when he would clean before company especially when he would clean rooms I had just done! He would even "joke" sometimes "Well, you would never win the Good Housekeeping seal of approval". I would feel like I wasn't good enough for him.

"You make me feel like a failure!" I would shout right before guests arrived. No dust in sight but tension you could cut with a knife. That certainly was not the comfortable home I was trying to create.

I have learned to own my method of cleaning. I have my definition of a guest- ready house and my husband has his version. If he chooses to clean after me I choose to not let it reflect on me. He has his comfort zone and I have mine. I do not need to feel less than because he prefers a spotless house for guests. His thoughts and feelings on the subject do not need to make me feel as though I have let him or anyone down by having less stringent boundaries.

We downsized a few years ago into a much smaller house. We enjoy entertaining but my husband often said the new house was too small for entertaining. We throw a Halloween open house every year. Our daughter invites her friends to trick or treat in our neighborhood and I invite their parents to hang out. There is food and drink and lots of conversation. One year, as everyone was leaving one of my friends said "That was the most fun I have had in a long time! Thank you so much for inviting me!" Later in the week, I made a point of mentioning her comment to my husband. He was pleasantly surprised. And he really heard me because it changed how he felt about his home. His thoughts on how things should be made him feel less than when we entertained. A voice in his head kept telling him that his home was not worthy. This is important: *the house wasn't creating this feeling.* He was making himself feel that way with his own thoughts on the subject.

If your mother makes a comment about your life and you, in response, internalize feelings of inferiority, it is important to remember that your mother did not make you feel that way. Your own thoughts about Mom, acceptable occupations, or lifestyle drove those feelings. And if your thoughts drove your feelings then it makes sense that if you were to craft new thoughts you could drive away those old feelings and create new ones. If you are living your authentic life, which makes you happy, then you will care much less what people say. Their judgments are on them, not you.

It helps to look at your feelings closely. They may be telling you something about your life you don't want to admit. Or they may just be an automatic reaction to inferred judgment, judgment that is entirely in your head. Your mother is not really telling you she doesn't approve of your life. She may just be worried. We only feel judged when we allow ourselves to feel judged. I no longer feel judged when my husband cleans rooms after I have just finished them - and to give him credit, he really doesn't do that much anymore. I know that his need to make the house look a certain way for others is his thing and I don't need to own any of it. If I were to pick the most important concept I learned about myself over the past twenty years it would be that I alone am responsible for how I feel and react.

References:

Carver, C.S., & Scheier, M.F. (2012). *Perspectives on Personality.* Upper Saddle River: Pearson.

Kurcinka, M.S. (2006). *Raising Your Spirited Child.* New York: HarperCollins Publishers.

Peterson, C. (2006). *A Primer on Positive Psychology.* New York: Oxford University Press.

Robin Schneider Larkin has been unlocking the doors to her authentic life for many years. She lives in Saratoga County, NY with her husband, daughter and dog. Currently at work on her Master's in Counseling she plans to graduate in 2017.

www.ingramcontent.com/pod-product-compliance
Lightning Source LLC
Chambersburg PA
CBHW060507080526
44584CB00015B/1582